VERMONT

The Green Mountain State

BY
JOHN HAMILTON

Abdo & Daughters
An imprint of Abdo Publishing | abdopublishing.com

abdopublishing.com

Published by ABDO Publishing, a division of ABDO, PO Box 398166, Minneapolis, Minnesota 55439. Copyright © 2017 by Abdo Consulting Group, Inc. International copyrights reserved in all countries. No part of this book may be reproduced in any form without written permission from the publisher. ABDO & Daughters™ is a trademark and logo of ABDO Publishing.

Printed in the United States of America, North Mankato, Minnesota.
072016
092016

Editor: Sue Hamilton   **Contributing Editor:** Bridget O'Brien
Graphic Design: Sue Hamilton
Cover Art Direction: Candice Keimig   **Cover Photo Selection:** Neil Klinepier
Cover Photo: iStock
Interior Images: 4 Corners New England, Abenaki, Alamy, Amtrak, AP, Dreamstime, Getty, Granger Collection, History.com, iStock, John Hamilton, Library of Congress, MFWills, Minden Pictures, Mile High Maps, Mountain High Maps, One Mile Up, Sandra Mansi, Stowe Derby, Trapp Family Lodge, U.S. Fish and Wildlife, Vermont Lake Monsters, Visit Barre, & Wikimedia.

Statistics: *State and City Populations*, U.S. Census Bureau, July 1, 2015 estimates; *Land and Water Area*, U.S. Census Bureau, 2010 Census, MAF/TIGER database; *State Temperature Extremes*, NOAA National Climatic Data Center; *Climatology and Average Annual Precipitation*, NOAA National Climatic Data Center, 1980-2015 statewide averages; *State Highest and Lowest Points*, NOAA National Geodetic Survey.

Websites: To learn more about the United States, visit booklinks.abdopublishing.com. These links are routinely monitored and updated to provide the most current information available.

Cataloging-in-Publication Data

Names: Hamilton, John, 1959- author.
Title: Vermont / by John Hamilton.
Description: Minneapolis, MN : Abdo Publishing, [2017] | Series: The United
    States of America | Includes index.
Identifiers: LCCN 2015957743 | ISBN 9781680783483 (lib. bdg.) |
    ISBN 9781680774528 (ebook)
Subjects: LCSH: Vermont--Juvenile literature.
Classification: DDC 974.3--dc23
LC record available at http://lccn.loc.gov/2015957743

CONTENTS

THE
GREEN MOUNTAIN
STATE

There are many ways to experience Vermont. There are long hiking paths through forested mountains. Winding country roads lead past dairy farms and quaint New England villages where time seems to stand still. In autumn, maple trees turn a riot of color, attracting "leaf peepers" from all over the country. In winter, the mountain slopes are filled with skiers hurtling downhill on fresh powder.

The people of Vermont have a well-known independent streak. The state was a self-ruling republic for 14 years, with its own constitution, before joining the Union in 1791. Vermont may be small, but its plucky citizens keep coming up with big ideas, from covered bridges and maple syrup, to snowboards and Ben & Jerry's ice cream.

The Green Mountains run north and south throughout the length of Vermont. The word "Vermont" is a combination of two French words (*verts monts*). The phrase means "green mountains." That is why Vermont is nicknamed "The Green Mountain State."

Vermont is famous for its covered bridges, such as Upper Falls Covered Bridge near Weathersfield.

QUICK FACTS

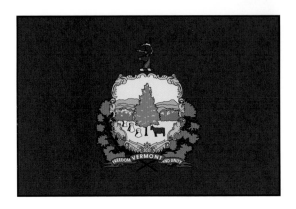

Name: Vermont is French (*verts monts*) for "green mountains."

State Capital: Montpelier, population 7,592

Date of Statehood: March 4, 1791 (14th state)

Population: 626,042 (49th-most populous state)

Area (Total Land and Water): 9,616 square miles (24,905 sq km), 45th-largest state

Largest City: Burlington, population 42,452

Nickname: The Green Mountain State

Motto: Freedom and Unity

Red Clover

State Bird: Hermit Thrush

State Flower: Red Clover

State Rock: Granite, Marble, and Slate

State Tree: Sugar Maple

State Song: "These Green Mountains"

Highest Point: Mount Mansfield, 4,393 feet (1,339 m)

Lowest Point: Lake Champlain, 95 feet (29 m)

Average July High Temperature: 78°F (26°C)

Record High Temperature: 105°F (41°C), in Vernon on July 4, 1911

Average January Low Temperature: 7°F (-14°C)

Record Low Temperature: -50°F (-46°C), in Bloomfield on December 30, 1933

Average Annual Precipitation: 46 inches (117 cm)

Number of U.S. Senators: 2

Number of U.S. Representatives: 1

U.S. Presidents Born in Vermont: Chester A. Arthur (1829-1886), Calvin Coolidge (1872-1933)

U.S. Postal Service Abbreviation: VT

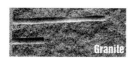

GEOGRAPHY

Vermont is part of a six-state region called New England. It is in the northeastern part of the United States. It is a small state, covering 9,616 square miles (24,905 sq km). It ranks just 45th in size among the states.

Vermont is shaped like a long triangle pointed southward. The state is about 157 miles (253 km) long from north-to-south, and 90 miles (145 km) east-to-west at its widest point near the Canadian border. It is just 42 miles (68 km) wide at the Massachusetts border in the south.

The south-flowing Connecticut River forms a long border with the state of New Hampshire to the east. To the south is Massachusetts. To the west is the state of New York. Vermont shares an international border with the country of Canada to the north. Vermont is the only New England state that does not border the Atlantic Ocean.

The Connecticut River flows between farmland in Newbury, Vermont, and Haverhill, New Hampshire.

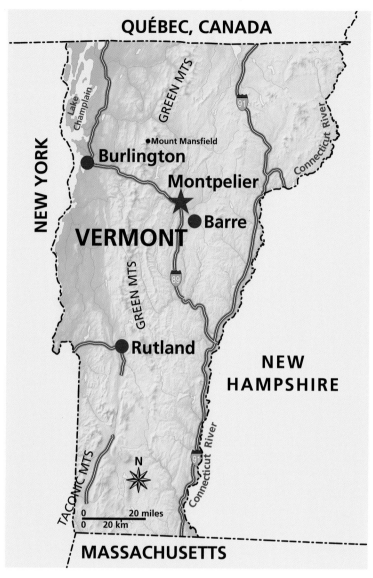

QUÉBEC, CANADA

NEW YORK

Lake Champlain

GREEN MTS

91

●Mount Mansfield

Burlington

Montpelier

●**Barre**

VERMONT

Connecticut River

GREEN MTS

89

●**Rutland**

NEW HAMPSHIRE

TACONIC MTS

N

Connecticut River

91

0   20 miles
0   20 km

MASSACHUSETTS

Vermont's total land and water area is 9,616 square miles (24,905 sq km). It is the 45th-largest state. The state capital is Montpelier.

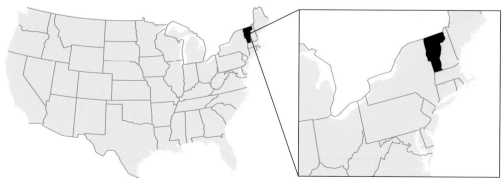

The Green Mountains run north and south through the middle of Vermont. They are part of the larger Appalachian Mountains, which stretch 1,500 miles (2,414 km) from Canada to the state of Alabama. They were formed more than 480 million years ago.

The Green Mountains probably got their name because of their green forests, but there are also many green-colored rocks, a kind of

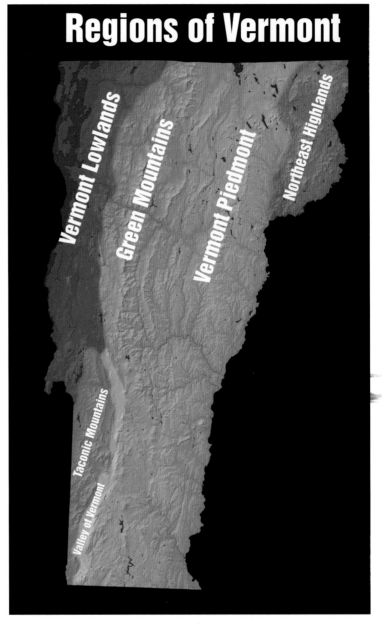

Regions of Vermont

Vermont Lowlands

Green Mountains

Vermont Piedmont

Northeast Highlands

Taconic Mountains

Valley of Vermont

shale, found in the mountains. Vermont's highest mountain is Mount Mansfield. It is in the northern part of the Green Mountains. It rises 4,393 feet (1,339 m) high.

The Taconic Mountains are in the southwestern part of Vermont. Like the Green Mountains, they are part of the Appalachian Mountains.

Quechee Gorge is Vermont's deepest gorge. It is in the Vermont Piedmont. The Ottauquechee River runs through it.

In northwestern Vermont are the Vermont Lowlands, also known as the Champlain Valley. This region has fertile soil that is good for farming. Lake Champlain is one of the largest lakes in the United States. Vermont shares the lake with New York to the west. Vermont's largest city, Burlington, is on the southeastern shore of Lake Champlain.

The narrow Valley of Vermont is sandwiched between the Green Mountains and the Taconic Mountains in the southwest. Marble and limestone quarries are found in this area.

East of the Green Mountains is the Vermont Piedmont region. There are many rolling hills and valleys. There are also some erosion-resistant, granite mountains that rise up above the surrounding countryside.

In the northeastern corner of Vermont is the Northeast Highlands region. It is also known as the Northeast Kingdom. It has rugged land filled with mountains, bogs, and forests of fir and spruce trees.

GEOGRAPHY

CLIMATE AND
WEATHER

Vermont has a humid continental climate, with four distinct seasons. There can be big swings in temperature. Summers are usually warm. Winters are cold, especially in the mountains. Large air masses from different parts of the continent often drift over Vermont. Warm, moist air arrives from the south. Colder, drier air drifts down from Canada. Cool, damp air also blows in from the nearby Atlantic Ocean to the east. When these weather systems collide, storms can develop.

Heavy rains from Tropical Storm Irene caused dangerous flooding in Waitsfield, Vermont, in 2011.

Snowboarders and skiers enjoy a winter storm near Stowe, Vermont.

In July, the average high temperature is 78°F (26°C). The record high occurred on July 4, 1911, in the town of Vernon. On that day, the thermometer rose to 105°F (41°C). The average January low temperature in Vermont is 7°F (-14°C). On December 30, 1933, in the town of Bloomfield, the temperature sank to a record low of -50°F (-46°C).

The average annual precipitation in Vermont is 46 inches (117 cm). Severe weather sometimes strikes the state, including blizzards and heavy thunderstorms. Tornados are rare, however.

CLIMATE AND WEATHER

PLANTS AND ANIMALS

Forests cover about 78 percent of Vermont. That is equal to roughly 4.6 million acres (1.9 million ha) of land. Most of Vermont's forests are on private property. Pine, spruce, and fir trees are common in the mountains. Deciduous trees are found in the lowlands, including beech, birch, and maple. Other trees growing in the state include alder, ash, aspen, basswood, butternut, cedar, cherry, oak, tamarack, and tupelo.

The sugar maple is Vermont's state tree. It accounts for close to 20 percent of the state's forests. Vermont is famous for the stunning fall colors of its trees, from vivid shades of red, yellow, and orange. People travel from all over the country to witness nature's colorful display.

Although Vermont is known more for its fall foliage, the state's forests and meadows are also filled with colorful wildflowers and shrubs. Spring blooms are especially beautiful. Favorite Vermont native wildflowers include Jack-in-the-pulpit, coltsfoot, and trout lilies. Red clover is the official state flower.

Flowers dot a Vermont hill.

People travel from all over to see the stunning fall colors of Vermont's trees.

Black Bear

Wildlife is plentiful in Vermont. There are 58 species of mammals scampering through the state's forests and meadows. They include beavers, black bears, coyotes, bobcats, chipmunks, rabbits, squirrels, fishers, gray foxes, long-tailed weasels, moose, raccoons, red foxes, striped skunks, and porcupines. White-tailed deer are found in abundance throughout Vermont. They live in forested mountain areas and near open fields. Their name comes from the white color of the underside of their tails.

There are more than 250 species of birds soaring through the blue skies of Vermont. Some of the most common include American goldfinches, American robins, barred owls, crows, common loons, eastern bluebirds, wild turkeys, ospreys, peregrine falcons, red-tailed hawks, ruby-throated hummingbirds, and ruffed grouse. The official state bird of Vermont is the hermit thrush.

The lakes and rivers of Vermont are teeming with more than 90 species of fish. They include largemouth and smallmouth bass, perch, pike, bullhead, shad, carp, rainbow trout, and muskellunge. The official state cold-water fish of Vermont is the brook trout. The official state warm-water fish is the walleye.

The painted turtle is Vermont's official state reptile.

Common reptiles and amphibians found scurrying and slithering in Vermont include blue-spotted salamanders, eastern newts, eastern red-back salamanders, spring peepers, painted turtles, wood turtles, five-lined skinks, milk snakes, garter snakes, eastern ribbonsnakes, and eastern rat snakes.

The only venomous snake in Vermont is the timber rattlesnake. Like all snakes, these reptiles are helpful to the state's ecosystems. They eat mice, voles, and rats. Although non-venomous snakes far outnumber venomous snakes in Vermont, hikers should take care when exploring. People should look carefully before stepping over logs or climbing rocky ledges.

PLANTS AND ANIMALS

HISTORY

Paleo-Indians hunted and fished in the Vermont area.

People moved into the Vermont area after the last Ice Age glaciers melted, approximately 10,000 to 12,000 years ago. These Paleo-Indians were the ancestors of today's Native Americans. By the time the first Europeans came to present-day Vermont in the 1500s, two Native American tribes dominated the area. They were the Iroquois and an Algonquin-speaking group called the Abenaki.

Vermont's Lake Champlain is named after French explorer Samuel de Champlain.

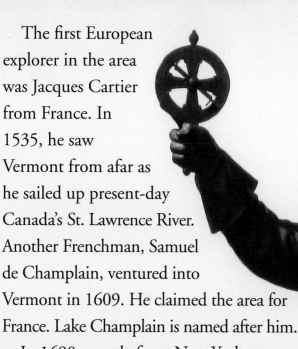

The first European explorer in the area was Jacques Cartier from France. In 1535, he saw Vermont from afar as he sailed up present-day Canada's St. Lawrence River. Another Frenchman, Samuel de Champlain, ventured into Vermont in 1609. He claimed the area for France. Lake Champlain is named after him.

In 1690, people from New York set up a trading post at Chimney Point, in northwestern Vermont. The British built Fort Dummer in southeastern Vermont in 1724. It was the first permanent European settlement in the state.

The French built powerful forts near Lake Champlain. Conflicts between the British and French caused the French and Indian War (1754-1763). Both sides wanted to control Lake Champlain. It was an important waterway for moving furs and other trade goods by boat. After years of fighting, the 1763 Treaty of Paris awarded the British all of the French land east of the Mississippi River, including Vermont.

After the French and Indian War, Vermont found itself in conflict with its powerful neighbor New York, which wanted Vermont's land. The citizens of Vermont did not want to be a part of New York. To protect themselves, they formed a powerful militia called the Green Mountain Boys. They were led by Vermont frontiersman Ethan Allen. The Green Mountain Boys kept New York from controlling Vermont's territory.

Ethan Allen and the Green Mountain Boys captured Fort Ticonderoga on May 10, 1775. They took cannons and other heavy weapons that the American forces needed.

When the Revolutionary War (1775-1783) erupted, the Green Mountain Boys played a very important part in the fight for freedom from Great Britain. Fort Ticonderoga was a British stronghold. It was located on the southern end of Lake Champlain, right across the border in New York. Led by Ethan Allen, a group of about 100 Green Mountain Boys and others daringly snuck into the fort on May 10, 1775. They overwhelmed the British defenders. Fort Ticonderoga contained dozens of cannons. The captured artillery pieces were later used by the Americans to force the British army to retreat from Boston, Massachusetts.

In 1777, Vermont declared that it was an independent nation. It called itself the Vermont Republic. Its state constitution was the first in America to give voting rights to all men. It also outlawed adult slavery, and required the creation of public schools. Fourteen years after its creation, the Vermont Republic joined the United States in 1791. It became the first state to join the Union after the original 13 colonies.

The Vermont Republic began at the Old Constitution House in Windsor, Vermont.

In September 1814, American forces defeated British warships on Lake Champlain in the Battle of Plattsburgh.

During the War of 1812 (1812-1815), American warships, plus Vermont and New York troops, defended against an invasion fleet of British ships on Lake Champlain. The British forces were defeated at the Battle of Plattsburgh in 1814.

During the 1800s, Vermont's farms and factories grew. Canals were built connecting Lake Champlain to the Hudson River. That meant Vermont could easily ship goods to large cities in New York and elsewhere. The first railroad began operating in the state in 1848, making it even easier to sell and transport products made in Vermont.

Most Vermont citizens opposed slavery. The Underground Railroad was very active in the state. Vermont's citizens helped many slaves escape to freedom in Canada and elsewhere.

When the Civil War (1861-1865) broke out, more than 34,000 Vermont men joined the Union North. They fought against the Confederate South, which wanted to keep slavery and break away from the Union. About 5,000 Vermont soldiers died or were wounded in the war.

In the 1900s, manufacturing became more important in Vermont. Fabric mills were built along swift-flowing rivers. Less land was used for agriculture, even though dairy farming remained strong.

Vermont's economy was hit hard by the Great Depression. It started in 1929 and lasted through much of the 1930s. Many people lost their jobs and homes. During America's involvement in World War II (1941-1945), the economy began to recover. Vermont farm products and factory goods were in demand. More than 50,000 people from Vermont served in the armed forces during the war.

After World War II, service industries became much more important to Vermont's economy, especially tourism. Today, ski resorts attract many visitors to the state. Others come to see Vermont's beautiful natural scenery and charming small towns.

Skiers flocked to the Snow Valley Ski Lodge in Winhall, Vermont, in 1939. Today, Vermont ski resorts continue to attract many visitors to the state.

HISTORY

DID YOU KNOW?

• Vermont has four seasons: winter, spring, summer, and autumn. Some say it also has a fifth season: mud. From late March to May, water from melting snow can't soak into the frozen ground. It makes many dirt and gravel roads so muddy that vehicles, people, cows, and horses often get stuck. Even paved roads become frosty and riddled with potholes.

• The film *The Sound of Music* is about the Trapp family from Austria. They escaped the forces of Nazi Germany just before the start of World War II (1939-1945). The musical film, which starred Julie Andrews and Christopher Plummer, won five Academy Awards, including Best Picture, in 1966. The real Trapp family eventually made their way to Vermont in the early 1940s. They said the Green Mountains reminded them of their home in Austria. They built the Trapp Family Lodge, which is a resort near the town of Stowe. Today, the lodge is run by surviving members and relatives of the Trapp family.

• There's a monster lurking beneath the waves of Lake Champlain. That's what some people believe. Tales of a lake monster date back to when Iroquois and Abenaki Native Americans were the only ones in the Vermont region. Some stories say that Samuel de Champlain, the French adventurer for whom the lake is named, spotted the fearsome creature while exploring Vermont. Over the years, hundreds of people claim they have seen the lake monster, which has a long neck and a mouth filled with rows of sharp teeth. It even has a nickname: Champ. What kind of creature is it? A giant eel, perhaps? Or a gar? Could it be a plesiosaur, a marine dinosaur that became extinct 65 million years ago? Or is it just a hoax? The search for Champ continues.

• Bennington Battle Day is a Vermont state holiday. It celebrates an American victory during the Revolutionary War in 1777. American soldiers, along with many of Vermont's Green Mountain Boys militia, defeated British invaders. A 300-foot (91-m) monument in the city of Bennington helps people remember the battle.

PEOPLE

Ethan Allen (1738-1789) was a frontiersman, soldier, and politician. He was born in Connecticut, but moved to the Vermont area after the French and Indian War (1754-1763). He led a militia called the Green Mountain Boys. They were farmers and pioneers who defended against land claims by neighboring New York. In 1775, during the Revolutionary War (1775-1783), Allen helped lead the Green Mountain Boys and other soldiers in capturing Fort Ticonderoga, a British stronghold near Lake Champlain. It was one of the first important victories of the war. Later that year, Allen was captured during an attack on Montreal, Canada. He was released in 1778. He returned home, where he worked to achieve statehood for Vermont.

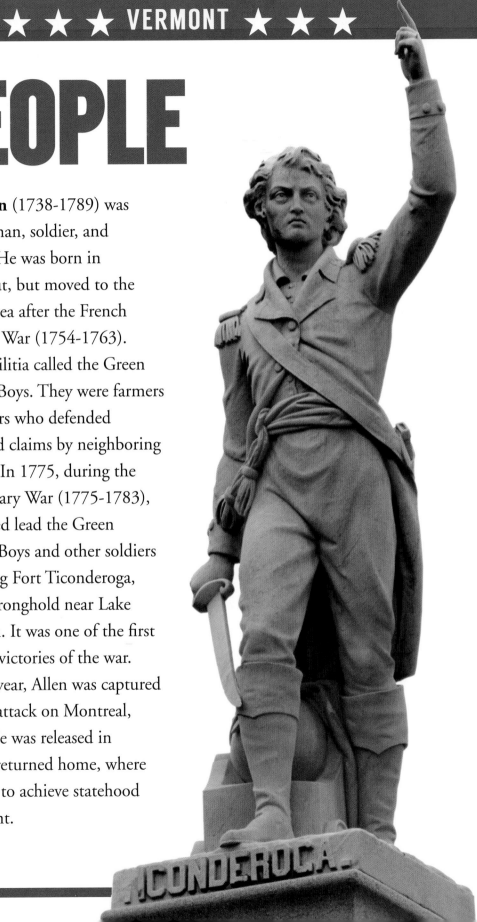

John Deere (1804-1886) was a blacksmith, inventor, and maker of farm equipment. He invented a self-scouring steel plow that was sturdy enough to handle the tough, sticky prairie sod of America's Great Plains. It was shaped so that the soil fell away as furrows were cut. Deere sold thousands of his plows to grateful farmers. The invention revolutionized agriculture and helped many pioneers settle the land. John Deere founded Deere and Company in 1837. Today, it remains one of the largest companies in the United States. John Deere was born in Rutland, Vermont.

George Dewey (1837-1917) was an officer of the United States Navy. He commanded American ships during the Spanish-American War of 1898. He became famous for his victory at the Battle of Manila Bay, in the Philippines. The battle was won without a single American combat death. Dewey returned home a hero. He was later promoted to Admiral of the Navy, the service's highest rank. No one else has ever held such a high rank in the U.S. Navy. Dewey was born in Montpelier, Vermont.

Elisha Graves Otis (1811-1861) invented the first automatic elevator brake in 1854. It keeps elevators from falling if the main cables break. The device made it safe for modern skyscrapers to be built many stories high. The Otis Elevator Company is still in business today. Otis also invented steam plows, bread-baking ovens, train brakes, and steam engines. He was born in Halifax, Vermont.

Hannah Teter (1987-) is an Olympic champion snowboarder. She was born in Belmont, Vermont. She started taking snowboarding lessons when she was just eight years old. She has won many Winter X Games, World Cup, and U.S. Open championships. At age 18, she won a gold medal in the half-pipe

competition at the 2006 Winter Olympic Games in Torino, Italy. She won a silver medal at the 2010 Winter Olympic Games in Vancouver, Canada. Teter uses her fame to perform charity work. She started a foundation called Hannah's Gold. It raises money to build schools and provide fresh water to poor villages in Africa and Central America.

CITIES

Montpelier is the capital of Vermont. Its population is about 7,592. It is the smallest state capital in the country. It is located in the north-central part of Vermont. It was named the state capital in 1805. Montpelier became a factory town in the mid-1800s. The Winooski River provided waterpower for fabric mills and iron foundries. Today, government is the city's main employer. There are also several insurance and granite processing companies. The Vermont College of Fine Arts offers degrees in writing, graphic design, music, and film. The current state capital building was completed in 1859. The gold-leaf dome is topped by a statue of Ceres, a Roman goddess of agriculture.

Burlington is the largest city in Vermont. Its population is about 42,452. However, neighboring cities, including South Burlington, Winooski, and Essex, give the metropolitan area a population of more than 210,000. Burlington is located along the eastern shore of Lake Champlain, in northwestern Vermont. The city's economy depends on education, health services, transportation, and light manufacturing. Burlington is home to the University of Vermont and Champlain College. The University of Vermont College of Medicine is one of the top-ranked medical schools in the nation. The ECHO Lake Aquarium and Science Center is home to more than 70 species of animals, including turtles, snakes, and fish. Ben & Jerry's ice cream got its start in Burlington in 1978.

CITIES

Rutland is the third-largest city in Vermont. Its population is about 15,824. It is located in the south-central part of the state, in the foothills of the Green Mountains. In the late-1800s, the city was one of the world's largest producers of marble. Its nickname used to be "Marble City." Today's businesses include health care, waste management, and aircraft parts manufacturing. The city is home to two colleges, the College of St. Joseph, and the Community College of Vermont. There are many buildings in the downtown area that are on the National Register of Historic Places. The Vermont State Fair is held in Rutland annually at the end of summer.

Barre is the fifth-largest city in Vermont. Pronounced "Bare-ee," its population is about 8,746. It is located in north-central Vermont, just southeast of the capital of nearby Montpelier. Barre is nicknamed "The Granite Center of the World." Local quarries produce top-quality granite that is used in monuments, statues, tombstones, and kitchen counters. Hope Cemetery contains more than 10,000 tombstones and memorials. All are made from gray granite chiseled from local quarries. Many of the monuments are unique works of art. The cemetery is a popular tourist destination.

TRANSPORTATION

There are 14,266 miles (22,959 km) of public roadways in Vermont. There are more than 2,700 bridges that are more than 20 feet (6 m) long. The two longest interstate highways include I-89 and I-91. They generally run north and south. Interstate I-89 passes through Burlington and the capital of Montpelier. Several ferries shuttle cars across Lake Champlain.

Vermont is famous for its covered wooden bridges. Built in the 1800s and early 1900s, the bridges were covered to keep the wood dry and prevent rot. Today, about 100 of these historic spans remain, scattered throughout the state. They are protected and preserved by state law.

There are 16 public-use airports in Vermont. The busiest is Burlington International Airport. It serves about 1.2 million passengers yearly.

The Windsor-Cornish Covered Bridge was built in 1866. With a length of 460 feet (140 km), it is one of the longest covered bridges in the United States. The bridge spans the Connecticut River, connecting Windsor, Vermont, with Cornish, New Hampshire.

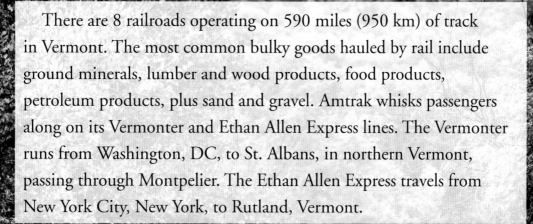

There are 8 railroads operating on 590 miles (950 km) of track in Vermont. The most common bulky goods hauled by rail include ground minerals, lumber and wood products, food products, petroleum products, plus sand and gravel. Amtrak whisks passengers along on its Vermonter and Ethan Allen Express lines. The Vermonter runs from Washington, DC, to St. Albans, in northern Vermont, passing through Montpelier. The Ethan Allen Express travels from New York City, New York, to Rutland, Vermont.

Amtrak's Ethan Allen Express winds its way through fall foliage in Castleton, Vermont.

NATURAL
RESOURCES

There are about 7,300 farms in Vermont. The average farm size is 171 acres (69 ha). In total, farms cover 1,250,000 acres (505,857 ha) of land. That is about 21 percent of Vermont's total land area.

The dairy industry has been cut back drastically since the 1940s. However, dairy farming is still an important part of Vermont's agriculture industry. The state's 131,000 dairy cows produce nearly $500 million in milk each year.

The top crops grown by Vermont farmers include hay and corn for feeding cattle. Apples, melons, sweet potatoes, and soybeans are also grown. Some apples are used to make cider and applesauce.

Vermont is by far the largest producer of pure maple syrup in the United States. The state harvested more than 1.4 million gallons (5.3 million l) of the sweet, sticky syrup in 2015. That is about 40 percent of the nation's total production.

A farmer checks the hoses that collect sap from maple trees in Randolph, Vermont. The state is by far the largest producer of pure maple syrup in the United States.

The E.L. Smith Quarry, near Barre, Vermont, is one of the largest and deepest granite quarries in the world. It is owned by the Rock of Ages Corporation. The quarry is a popular tourist destination.

Forests cover about 78 percent of Vermont. Wood that is logged from Vermont forests is used to make furniture, cabinets, plywood, and many other products.

Vermont is one of the nation's leading centers for marble and granite quarrying. Some of the deepest and most productive quarries in the world are located near the cities of Barre and Rutland. Vermont is also a big producer of slate.

NATURAL RESOURCES

INDUSTRY

Vermont has hundreds of manufacturing companies scattered throughout the state. Most are small, producing specialized products. However, Vermont has attracted several computer and electronics manufacturers, especially in the Burlington and Rutland areas. GlobalFoundries operates a large semiconductor production plant in Essex Junction.

Vermont factories make products that are known all over the country. Food lovers enjoy Ben & Jerry's ice cream and Bruegger's Bagels. Orvis is a sporting equipment and clothing business based in Sunderland. Burton Snowboards and Rome Snowboard Design Syndicate are both well-known Vermont sellers of winter sports equipment.

Ben & Jerry's ice cream is produced in Vermont. The ice cream factory tour is a popular tourist attraction.

Burton Snowboards was started by Jake Burton Carpenter in 1977. Today, the Burlington, Vermont, business is one of the top snowboard companies in the country.

Like many states today, much of Vermont's economy depends on the service industry. Instead of making products, companies in the service industry sell services to other businesses and consumers. It includes businesses such as banking, financial services, health care, insurance, restaurants, and tourism. About 62 percent of people working in Vermont are employed in the service industry.

Tourism is a huge industry in Vermont. Visitors enjoy the Green Mountains, stunning fall colors, ski resorts, and quiet small towns. Tourists spend more than $1.8 billion in the state each year, enough to support more than 30,000 jobs.

INDUSTRY

SPORTS

There are no professional major league sports teams in Vermont. The Vermont Lake Monsters are a popular Minor League Baseball (MiLB) team. Named after the legendary creature that lurks beneath the waves of Lake Champlain, the team plays its home games in Burlington.

People travel from all over the country to enjoy winter sports in Vermont. There are many world-class ski resorts nestled in the Green Mountains. Some of Vermont's most popular skiing destinations include Stowe Mountain Resort, Sugarbush Resort, Smugglers' Notch, Killington Ski Resort, Jay Peak, and Burke Mountain.

For cross-country skiers, the Catamount Trail stretches 300 miles (483 km) across the entire length of Vermont. The Stowe Derby is the oldest downhill/cross-country ski race in North America. Competitors race on one pair of skis from the top of Mount Mansfield (Vermont's highest peak) to the village of Stowe. The racing tradition began in 1945.

Racers take off on the Stowe Derby ski race. Skiers enjoy the challenge of using only one pair of skis in the downhill/ cross-country race.

Popular summer sports in Vermont include golfing, biking, hiking, rock climbing, hunting, and fishing. The Long Trail is a 272-mile (438-km) -long hiking path that follows the ridges of the Green Mountains down the length of the entire state from north to south. Called Vermont's "footpath in the wilderness," the trail's construction was completed in 1930. It is the oldest long-distance hiking trail in the country.

Hikers on Vermont's Long Trail.

ENTERTAINMENT

Vermont is home to many museums and historic sites. The Ethan Allen Homestead Museum is in Burlington. It preserves the farmhouse where the famous Vermont frontiersman lived before his death in 1789. Inside the museum, visitors can learn about the daily skills pioneers mastered in order to survive on the rugged Vermont frontier.

The birthplace and boyhood home of President Calvin Coolidge is a National Historic Landmark in Plymouth Notch, Vermont. The Marsh-Billings-Rockefeller National Historical Park is near Woodstock, Vermont. The park's beautiful landscapes are the result of scientifically managed forests and farmlands.

Ethan Allen Homestead Museum

The Vermont Theatre Company is in Brattleboro. It holds an annual Shakespeare in the Park summer production that attracts thousands of picnickers to Brattleboro's Living Memorial Park. The Vermont Symphony Orchestra is based in Burlington. It performs classical works throughout the state.

The people of Vermont love festivals. Some of the most popular include the Vermont Apple Festival in Springfield, the Vermont Maple Festival in St. Albans, the Green Mountain Film Festival in Montpelier, and the Middlebury Festival on the Green, which features musical acts from all over the region.

The popular Vermont State Fair is held each summer in Rutland. Started in 1846, the fair today includes thrill rides, animal exhibits, musical acts, and a demolition derby.

People enjoy a ride at the Vermont State Fair.

TIMELINE

10,000-8,000 BC—The first Paleo-Indians arrive in the Vermont region.

1500s—Abenaki and Iroquois Native Americans inhabit the Vermont area.

1609—Explorer Samuel de Champlain claims the Vermont area for France.

1724—The British build Fort Dummer, the first permanent European settlement in Vermont.

1763—The British gain control of the Vermont area after the French and Indian War.

1775—Vermont militia Green Mountain Boys capture Fort Ticonderoga.

1777—Vermont declares itself an independent republic.

1791—Vermont becomes the 14th state in the Union.

1861-1865—About 34,000 people from Vermont serve in the Civil War.

1927—Major flooding in Vermont causes many deaths and destruction.

1930s—Tourism starts to become an important industry for Vermont.

1941-1945—More than 50,000 people from Vermont serve in World War II.

2011—Tropical Storm Irene causes statewide flooding, resulting in three deaths and hundreds of millions of dollars in damage.

2016—Vermont Senator Bernard "Bernie" Sanders runs for president. Although losing the nomination to fellow Democrat Hillary Clinton, Sanders remains an extremely popular politician, especially among young people.

GLOSSARY

COVERED BRIDGES

Usually made of wood, covered bridges have enclosed sides and a roof, which greatly protect the structure. Some are strong enough to support trains.

DECIDUOUS

A tree or other plant that sheds its leaves each autumn.

GLACIERS

Huge, slow-moving sheets of ice that grow and shrink as the climate changes. During the Ice Age, some glaciers covered entire regions and measured more than one mile (1.6 km) thick.

GREAT DEPRESSION

A time in American history beginning in 1929 and lasting for several years when many businesses failed and millions of people lost their jobs. The Great Depression finally eased in the mid-1930s, but didn't end until many countries entered World War II, around 1939.

ICE AGE

A geological period of cold climate, with thick sheets of ice and snow covering the polar regions and expanding over the continents. The last major Ice Age peaked approximately 20,000 years ago.

IROQUOIS

A powerful alliance of Native American tribes, including the Cayuga, Mohawk, Oneida, Onondaga, Seneca, and Tuscarora people.

Lake Champlain

A large lake that lies between Vermont and New York. It is about 120 miles (193 km) long and covers 435 square miles (1,127 sq km). Named for French explorer Samuel de Champlain, the lake has more than 70 islands, and is home to 81 species of fish.

Marble

A rock that is prized for sculptures, monuments, and buildings. It is a type of limestone. It is found in great abundance in Vermont's Green Mountains.

Militia

A group of people who perform part-time military duties. Instead of serving full-time, they are called up for service when needed.

Piedmont

A large region that is adjacent to mountains. The word *piedmont* means "at the foot of the mountains."

Revolutionary War

The war fought between the American colonies and Great Britain from 1775-1783. It is also known as the War of Independence or the American Revolution.

Underground Railroad

In the early- to mid-1800s, people created the Underground Railroad to help African Americans escape from slave states. Not an actual railroad, it was instead a secret network of safe houses and connecting routes that led slaves to freedom.

World War II

A conflict that was fought from 1939 to 1945, involving countries around the world. The United States entered the war after Japan bombed the American naval base at Pearl Harbor, in Oahu, Hawaii, on December 7, 1941.

INDEX